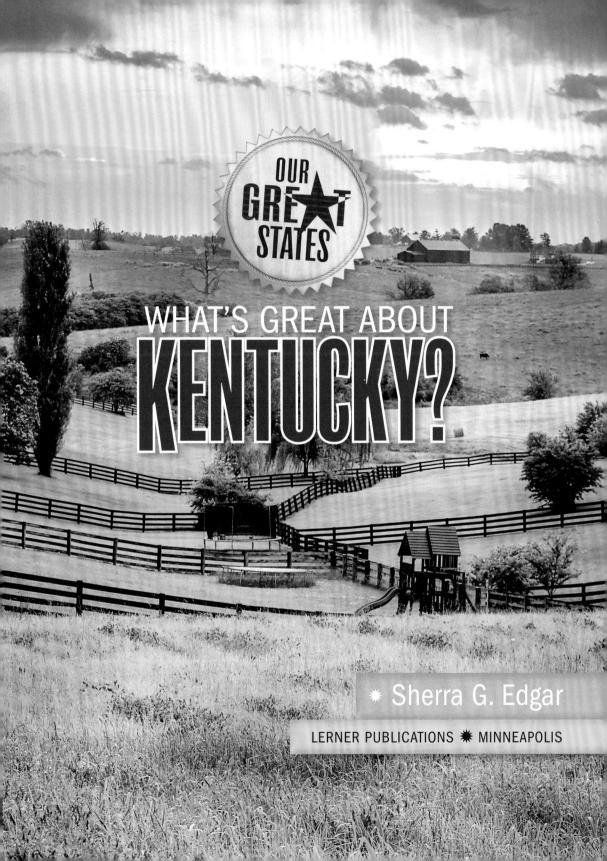

OUR
GRE★T
STATES

WHAT'S GREAT ABOUT
KENTUCKY?

★ Sherra G. Edgar

LERNER PUBLICATIONS ★ MINNEAPOLIS

CONTENTS

KENTUCKY WELCOMES YOU! ✳ 4

Copyright © 2016
by Lerner Publishing Group, Inc.

Content Consultant: Thomas H. Appleton Jr.,
PhD, Professor of History, Eastern Kentucky
University

Lerner Publications Company
A division of Lerner Publishing Group, Inc.
241 First Avenue North
Minneapolis, MN 55401 USA

For reading levels and more information, look
up this title at www.lernerbooks.com.

Main body text set in ITC Franklin Gothic Std
Book Condensed 12/15.
Typeface provided by Adobe Systems.

**Library of Congress Cataloging-in-Publication
Data**

Edgar, Sherra G.
      What's great about Kentucky? / Sherra
G. Edgar.
          pages   cm. — (Our great states)
      ISBN 978-1-4677-3878-1 (lb : alk. paper)
      ISBN 978-1-4677-8501-3 (pb : alk. paper)
      ISBN 978-1-4677-8502-0 (eb pdf)
      1. Kentucky—Juvenile literature.
  2. Kentucky—Guidebooks—Juvenile
literature. I. Title.
F451.3.E34 2015
976.9—dc23   2015000563

Manufactured in the United States of America
1 – PC – 7/15/15

KENTUCKY Welcomes You!

Welcome to Kentucky, the Bluegrass State! The state is known for all of its horse racing attractions. Join in the fun by visiting the site of the famous Kentucky Derby. Or check out the state's many national and state parks. There is plenty of wildlife to see and trails to explore. If you're looking for adventure, be sure to stop at Kentucky Kingdom to enjoy some amusement park rides. As you make your way through the state, you'll learn about presidents, pioneers, and baseball. There is something for everyone in Kentucky. Keep reading to learn about the top ten things that make this state great!

Explore Kentucky's horse racing tracks and all the places in between! Just turn the page to find out all about the BLUEGRASS STATE. >

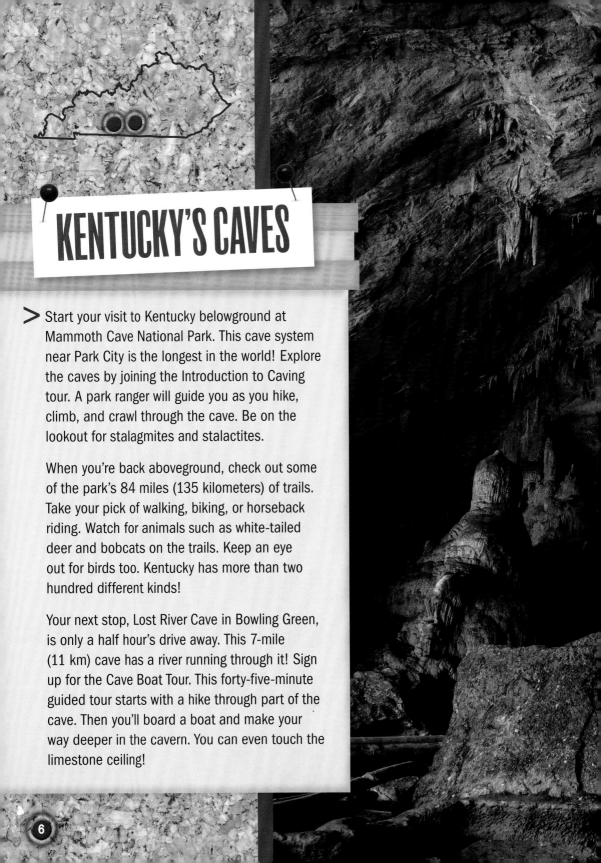

KENTUCKY'S CAVES

> Start your visit to Kentucky belowground at Mammoth Cave National Park. This cave system near Park City is the longest in the world! Explore the caves by joining the Introduction to Caving tour. A park ranger will guide you as you hike, climb, and crawl through the cave. Be on the lookout for stalagmites and stalactites.

When you're back aboveground, check out some of the park's 84 miles (135 kilometers) of trails. Take your pick of walking, biking, or horseback riding. Watch for animals such as white-tailed deer and bobcats on the trails. Keep an eye out for birds too. Kentucky has more than two hundred different kinds!

Your next stop, Lost River Cave in Bowling Green, is only a half hour's drive away. This 7-mile (11 km) cave has a river running through it! Sign up for the Cave Boat Tour. This forty-five-minute guided tour starts with a hike through part of the cave. Then you'll board a boat and make your way deeper in the cavern. You can even touch the limestone ceiling!

You can search different parts of Lost River Cave on your kayak.

BOWLING GREEN

Bowling Green is located in southern Kentucky. Pioneers started the city in 1798. The city's pioneers grew many crops, including strawberries. Many residents in the city do not farm anymore. Instead, the city is a center for business and education. The city is now the third largest in the state.

ABRAHAM LINCOLN BIRTHPLACE

> Travel to the Abraham Lincoln Birthplace National Historical Park in Hodgenville. The park includes two farms that Abraham Lincoln lived on as a child. Begin your trip at the park's visitor center. Here you'll learn about Lincoln's family and the lives of other early pioneers. The center has several historic items, such as the Lincoln family's Bible. Before you head outside, watch a short movie about Lincoln's early years in Kentucky.

Next, take a tour of the Memorial Building. The building is at the top of a staircase. The staircase's fifty-six steps represent the fifty-six years of Lincoln's life. At the Memorial, you'll see a model of the cabin in which Lincoln was born. It is believed to include some of the wood from the original cabin. The cabin has only one room and is full of clothes and items like the ones the Lincolns used.

ABRAHAM LINCOLN

Lincoln was born in a log cabin in Kentucky on February 12, 1809. In the 1800s, slavery was allowed in more than a dozen states, including Kentucky. Although the Lincolns lived in Kentucky, they were against slavery. When Abraham Lincoln was around seven years old, the family decided to leave the state. Later, when Lincoln became president, he worked to end slavery. In 1863, he issued the Emancipation Proclamation, which freed many slaves in the United States.

This log cabin at the Abraham Lincoln Birthplace is a model of the one in which Lincoln was born.

OWENSBORO

> Next, stop in Owensboro on the Ohio River. Come hungry! This city calls itself the Barbecue Capital of the World. If you're visiting in May, visit the International Bar-B-Q Festival. Be sure to try some of the barbecued meats. Vote for your favorites. Or sign up for the pie-eating contest. Maybe you'll be one of the lucky winners!

Owensboro is also known for its great music. Learn more about the music scene at the International Bluegrass Music Museum. Follow the timeline on the wall to see where bluegrass started. Then explore exhibits showing common bluegrass instruments such as a banjo. Walk through the Hall of Fame to see pictures of important musicians. You'll hear music throughout your visit. Maybe you'll have a new favorite song by the time you leave the museum! Two big music festivals are also held in Owensboro each summer. Check out the Big O Music Fest and ROMP. Many famous country and bluegrass singers perform at these festivals.

The bluegrass band G2 from Sweden performs at the annual ROMP festival.

Try different kinds of barbecued foods at the International Bar-B-Q Festival.

KENTUCKY DERBY MUSEUM

> Meet you at the races! Horse racing is a big attraction in Kentucky. A must-see stop on your trip is Churchill Downs in Louisville. This horse track is home to the annual Kentucky Derby horse race.

Start your day at the Kentucky Derby Museum at Churchill Downs. Watch a video to learn more about the history of the Kentucky Derby. Then see what it's like to be a jockey. Jump on a model horse and hold on tight! It's a quick two-minute ride to the finish line. After your race, have your picture taken in the Winner's Circle. Next, make your way to the second floor of the museum. Learn about the life of racing horses from the time they are born until their racing days. Don't forget to try on sample jockey clothing!

After exploring the museum, head outside for tours of the grounds. The walking tour takes you right to the horses. Then make your way through the paddock and learn fun facts from your guide along the way. Or sign up for the Inside the Gates tour. You'll get to see private areas of Churchill Downs, including the dining room and the lounge.

Try on a jockey jacket or see jackets and caps worn by past winners at the Kentucky Derby Museum.

HISTORY OF THE DERBY

The Kentucky Derby is a horse race held on the first Saturday of May each year. The first Kentucky Derby was held in 1857 on John and Henry Churchill's land. This land was later sold and named Churchill Downs after the two men. During the Kentucky Derby, horses and their jockeys race on a 1.25-mile (2 km) track. A horse named Secretariat ran the fastest race ever in 1973. He finished the race in 1:59 minutes!

13

LOUISVILLE SLUGGER
MUSEUM & FACTORY

> Continue your Louisville visit at the Louisville Slugger Museum & Factory. Here you'll learn all about the famous Louisville Slugger baseball bat. Players have used this brand for more than one hundred years!

Have your photo taken outside the museum, next to the world's biggest baseball bat. It weighs 68,000 pounds (30,840 kilograms). Then head inside the museum. Here you can climb on a giant stone baseball glove or practice your swing in the batting cages. Learn how the first Louisville bat was made in 1884, and see old baseball gear from famous players.

End your visit with a guided tour of the factory. See how Louisville Slugger bats are made. You'll learn every step in the process. After the tour, be sure to get your own free miniature bat! As you leave the museum and walk down Main Street, check out the Walk of Fame. It is full of plaques with the names and stories of famous players.

See Louisville Slugger bats signed by famous professional players.

The world's biggest baseball bat stands 120 feet (37 meters) tall!

LOUISVILLE ZOO

Pet and feed animals at the Louisville Zoo.

> Make your way to the Louisville Zoo next. The zoo is home to more than fifteen hundred animals! Start your trip at Glacier Run. Here you'll see polar and grizzly bears. Then watch the sea lions swim and play in the pool. You can also talk to zookeepers about animal life in cold weather.

Next, go to Gorilla Forest to see gorillas and other animals. Begin with a search through the treetop boardwalk. Watch gorillas from above and learn more about their habits. Look for knuckle prints from these big, hairy animals. Then come down from the treetops and see other African animals at the zoo. Listen for an elephant's trumpet and a lion's roar!

If you're looking for adventure, try out the zoo's ropes course. You'll be able to see the animals from up in the air! Try out all eighteen challenges on the course. When you're back on the ground, take a train ride around the zoo. Wave to the animals as you end your visit!

Watch and take pictures of the orangutans climbing around.

KENTUCKY KINGDOM

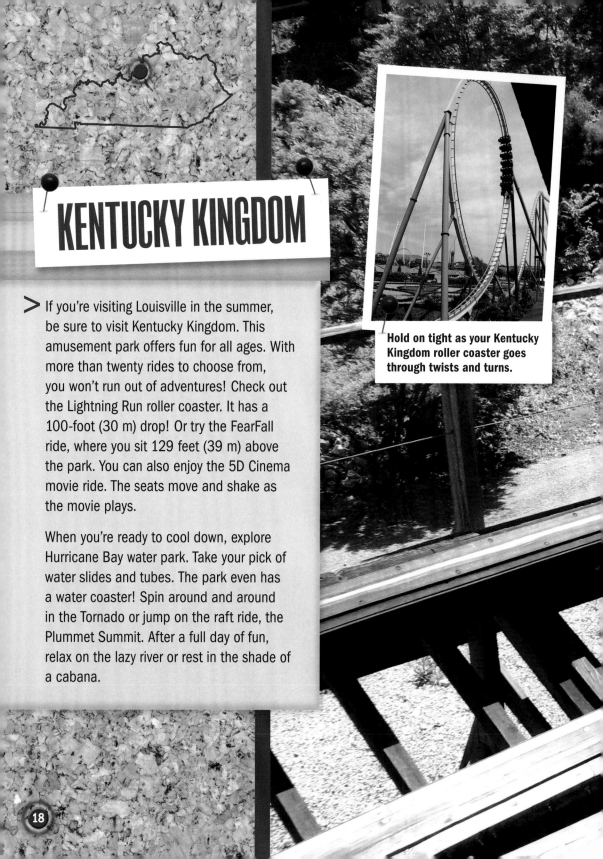

Hold on tight as your Kentucky Kingdom roller coaster goes through twists and turns.

> If you're visiting Louisville in the summer, be sure to visit Kentucky Kingdom. This amusement park offers fun for all ages. With more than twenty rides to choose from, you won't run out of adventures! Check out the Lightning Run roller coaster. It has a 100-foot (30 m) drop! Or try the FearFall ride, where you sit 129 feet (39 m) above the park. You can also enjoy the 5D Cinema movie ride. The seats move and shake as the movie plays.

When you're ready to cool down, explore Hurricane Bay water park. Take your pick of water slides and tubes. The park even has a water coaster! Spin around and around in the Tornado or jump on the raft ride, the Plummet Summit. After a full day of fun, relax on the lazy river or rest in the shade of a cabana.

How many waterslides will you ride at Hurricane Bay?

CUMBERLAND GAP

> The Cumberland Gap is located on the Kentucky-Virginia border. The Gap is a small opening through the Cumberland Mountains. Many American pioneers, including Abraham Lincoln's grandfather, used the Cumberland Gap trail to travel west beginning in the 1700s. They were moving west to claim land for farms. The pioneers used the Cumberland Gap because it was an easier path than going over the mountains.

Start your visit to the Gap at the visitor center. Stop in the Pioneer Playhouse and try on some pioneer clothing! Pack a bag with the help of workers dressed as pioneers. They'll tell you all about pioneer life. Then check out the museum. Touch real animal skins and see tools from the early 1800s.

Visitors to the Cumberland Gap can also hike more than 80 miles (129 km) of trails. Look for cool rock shapes and streams. You might also see deer, beavers, bobcats, and birds! After exploring on foot, hop in the car with your family. Drive up the mountain to Pinnacle Overlook. Here you'll get a great view of Kentucky, Virginia, and Tennessee!

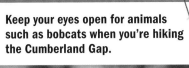
Keep your eyes open for animals such as bobcats when you're hiking the Cumberland Gap.

DANIEL BOONE
Daniel Boone was an explorer and pioneer. He is known for widening the Cumberland Gap path between Virginia and Kentucky. This path provided Americans with a way to move farther west. Boone lived much of his life in Kentucky. This skilled survivor and soldier loved adventure.

KENTUCKY LAKE

> Spend a day on Kentucky Lake along the Tennessee River. This large human-made lake covers 160,300 acres (65,000 hectares) of the state. Enjoy boating, swimming, camping, and more at this fun spot!

Kentucky Lake is also a great place for fishing. Huge white bass, smallmouth buffalo, and yellow perch have been caught in this lake. Watch or participate in one of many fishing tournaments in the area. Or rent a boat and explore the lake on your own. How many kinds of fish can you catch?

Kentucky Lake is a part of the Land Between the Lakes National Recreation Area. Here you can visit the Nature Station to see many animals that call Kentucky home. You might see great horned owls, coyotes, bison, or the red wolf. Then make your way to the Golden Pond Planetarium. The planetarium has a large dome that shows the night sky. Watch one of three astronomy shows or look through a telescope to see stars up close.

Which stars and planets will you see through a telescope at Golden Pond Planetarium?

Learn more about Kentucky Lake's animals on a guided tour of its nature trails.

SHAKER VILLAGE
OF PLEASANT HILL

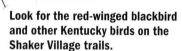

Look for the red-winged blackbird and other Kentucky birds on the Shaker Village trails.

> Make your last stop in Kentucky at Shaker Village of Pleasant Hill in Harrodsburg. This living-history museum teaches visitors about Shakers, a religious group that lived in Kentucky in the 1800s. Visit and tour some of the thirty-four buildings. You can see family homes and meeting houses. Watch workers in traditional clothing perform their everyday chores.

Stop at the farm to pet the farm animals. Then make your way to the trails. You can check out more than 30 miles (48 km) of trails on foot, on a bike, or on a horse. Be sure to grab a bird checklist in the village to take along on your journey. How many different birds will you see? After roaming the trails, enjoy a boat ride on the Kentucky River. Your guide will tell you about the river and its importance to the Shakers.

Explore the traditional Shaker kitchen at Shaker Village of Pleasant Hill.

YOUR TOP TEN!

You have read about ten amazing things to see and do in Kentucky. Think about what your Kentucky top ten list would include. What would you like to see if you visit the state? Would you want to hike, explore history, or see horses? What activities are most exciting to you? What would you tell your friends to do if they visited Kentucky? Keep these things in mind as you make your own top ten list.

KENTUCKY BY MAP

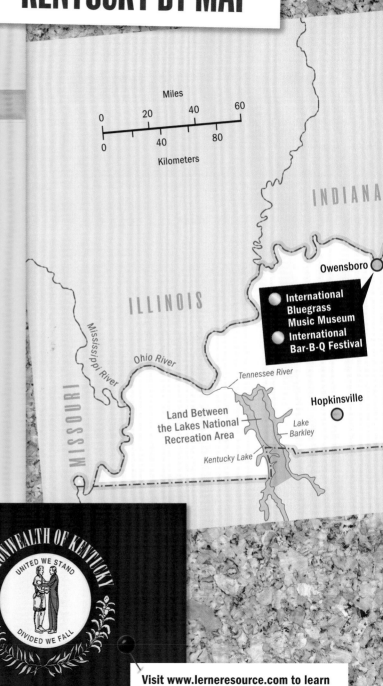

MAP KEY

⭐ Capital city

◯ City

◯ Point of interest

▲ Highest elevation

–·– State border

Miles

0   20   40   60

0   40   80

Kilometers

INDIANA

ILLINOIS

Mississippi River

Ohio River

Tennessee River

MISSOURI

Owensboro

International Bluegrass Music Museum

International Bar-B-Q Festival

Hopkinsville

Land Between the Lakes National Recreation Area

Lake Barkley

Kentucky Lake

COMMONWEALTH OF KENTUCKY

UNITED WE STAND

DIVIDED WE FALL

Visit www.lerneresource.com to learn more about the state flag of Kentucky.

OHIO

Covington

Florence

Ohio River

WEST VIRGINIA

Big Sandy River

Tug Fork River

- Churchill Downs
- Kentucky Derby Museum
- Louisville Slugger Museum & Factory
- Louisville Zoo
- Kentucky Kingdom

Georgetown

Frankfort

Louisville

N

Lexington

Shaker Village of Pleasant Hill (Harrodsburg)

Richmond

Kentucky River

CUMBERLAND PLATEAU

Elizabethtown

Abraham Lincoln Birthplace National Historical Park (Hodgenville)

Cumberland Gap National Historical Park

VIRGINIA

Mammoth Cave National Park (Mammoth Cave)

Bowling Green

Park City

Cumberland River

Big Black Mountain (4,145 feet/ 1,263 m)

C U M B E R L A N D   M O U N T A I N S

Lost River Cave

Cumberland Gap

TENNESSEE

KENTUCKY FACTS

NICKNAME: The Bluegrass State

SONG: "My Old Kentucky Home" by Stephen Collins Foster

MOTTO: "United We Stand, Divided We Fall"

> FLOWER: goldenrod

TREE: tulip poplar

BIRD: cardinal

ANIMAL: gray squirrel

> FOOD: blackberry

DATE AND RANK OF STATEHOOD: June 1, 1792; the 15th state

> CAPITAL: Frankfort

AREA: 40,411 square miles (104,664 sq. km)

AVERAGE JANUARY TEMPERATURE: 34°F (1°C)

AVERAGE JULY TEMPERATURE: 77°F (25°C)

POPULATION AND RANK: 4,395,295; 26th (2013)

MAJOR CITIES AND POPULATIONS: Louisville (609,893), Lexington (308,428), Bowling Green (61,488), Owensboro (58,416), Covington (40,956)

NUMBER OF US CONGRESS MEMBERS: 6 representatives, 2 senators

NUMBER OF ELECTORAL VOTES: 8

NATURAL RESOURCES: coal, limestone, natural gas, petroleum

> AGRICULTURAL PRODUCTS: corn, hay, hogs, horses, milk, wheat

MANUFACTURED GOODS: chemicals, processed food and beverages, automobiles

STATE HOLIDAYS AND CELEBRATIONS: Kentucky Derby Festival, Festival of the Bluegrass

GLOSSARY

bluegrass: traditional American music that is played with stringed instruments

cabana: a small building or tent that is often used at a swimming pool

exhibit: an object or collection that has been put on public display

jockey: someone who rides horses in races

paddock: an enclosed area at a racetrack where horses are kept before a race

pioneer: a person who goes to live in an unknown place where usually there are few or no people

stalactite: a pointed piece of rock that hangs down from the roof of a cave

stalagmite: a pointed piece of rock that sticks up from the floor of a cave

LERNER
SOURCE

Expand learning beyond the printed book. Download free, complementary educational resources for this book from our website, www.lernerresource.com.

FURTHER INFORMATION

Gosman, Gillian. *Abraham Lincoln*. New York: PowerKids Press, 2011. This book covers the life of the sixteenth president.

Kallio, Jamie. *What's Great about Virginia?* Minneapolis: Lerner Publications, 2015. Learn more about Kentucky's neighboring state, Virginia.

Kentucky Kids Pages
http://www.lrc.ky.gov/kidspages/kids.htm
At this fun site, you can find fun facts about Kentucky's government, play games, and watch videos.

Mammoth Cave National Park Trading Cards
http://www.nps.gov/maca/forkids/tradingcards.htm
Learn more about the Civil War and civil rights in Kentucky with these printable trading cards.

WebRangers
http://www.nps.gov/webrangers
Play games, do activities, and learn more about national parks and monuments, including those found in Kentucky.

Wilbur, Helen L. *D is for Derby: A Kentucky Derby Alphabet*. Ann Arbor, MI: Sleeping Bear, 2014. This book about the Kentucky Derby features famous winners and horses and a history of the event.

INDEX

PHOTO ACKNOWLEDGMENTS

The images in this book are used with the permission of: © Alexey Stiop/Shutterstock Images, pp. 1, 20–21; NASA, pp. 2–3; © American Spirit/Shutterstock Images, p. 4; © Amy Nichole Harris/Shutterstock Images, p. 5 (top); © Laura Westlund/Independent Picture Service, pp. 5 (bottom), 26; © kikujungboy/Shutterstock Images, pp. 6–7; © Austin Anthony/Daily News/AP Images, p. 7 (top); Lewis Wickes Hine/Library of Congress, p. 7 (bottom) (LC-DIG-nclc-00434); National Park Service, pp. 8–9, 9; Anthony Berger/Library of Congress, p. 8 (LC-DIG-ppmsca-19305); © Robert Bruck/KRT/Newscom, pp. 10–11; © Purestock/Thinkstock, p. 11 (bottom); © John Dunham/The Messenger-Inquirer/AP Images, p. 11 (top); © Mark Cornelison/MCT/Newscom, pp. 12–13; © dmac/Alamy, p. 13 (top); Detroit Publishing Co./Library of Congress, p. 13 (bottom) (LC-DIG-det-4a06266); © Brian Cahn/ZumaPress/Newscom, pp. 14–15; © Irina Mos/Shutterstock Images, p. 15 (right); © Lou Oms CC 2.0, p. 15 (left); © jdj150 CC 2.0, pp. 16–17; © wanderluster/iStockphoto, p. 16; © Richard Wong/Alamy, p. 17; © Jeremy Thompson CC 2.0, pp. 18-19, 18, 19; © mlorenz/Shutterstock Images, p. 21 (left); Alonzo Chappel, p. 21 (right); © Anne Kitzman/Shutterstock Images, pp. 22–23; © Daniel Dempster Photography/Alamy, p. 22; © Paul Cannon/Alamy, p. 23; © Clay Jackson/The Advocate Messenger/AP Images, pp. 24–25; © FloridaStock/Shutterstock Images, p. 24; © Age Fotostock/Alamy, p. 25; © nicoolay/iStockphoto, p. 26; © Elenathewise/iStockphoto, p. 29 (top); © 4maksym/iStockphoto, p. 29 (middle left); © alexeys/iStockphoto, p. 29 (middle right); © jeka1984/iStockphoto, p. 29 (bottom).

Front cover: © Kenneth Sponsler/Shutterstock.com (Cumberland Gap); © iStockphoto.com/truchb28 (Louisville Slugger factory); © Rob Carr/Getty Images (Kentucky Derby); © Laura Westlund/Independent Picture Service (map); © iStockphoto.com/fpm (seal); © iStockphoto.com/vicm (pushpins); © iStockphoto.com/benz190 (corkboard).